Hostage to the Empire!

Grand Moff Hissa clutched Ken.

"Let go of me!" the Jedi Prince shouted, as Hissa pressed a laserblaster against the boy's chin. Ken stopped squirming and held very still.

Hearing Ken's shout for help, Luke hurriedly pushed two stormtroopers aside and pointed his lightsaber at the grand moff, ready to put an end to Hissa as swiftly as he had destroyed the attacking giant Fefze beetles.

"Drop your weapon, or I'll destroy the boy—now!" Grand Moff Hissa exclaimed.

Luke hesitated. Then he retracted his lightsaber and dropped the weapon to the ground.

"Very good, Skywalker," Hissa said, gnashing his pointed teeth. "Now prepare to join your master, Obi-Wan Kenobi, in the world beyond!"

MISSION FROM MOUNT YODA

The Adventure Continues . . .

Also available in the STAR WARS® series, and published by Bantam Books:

THE GLOVE OF DARTH VADER
THE LOST CITY OF THE JEDI
ZORBA THE HUTT'S REVENGE

Forthcoming:

QUEEN OF THE EMPIRE
PROPHETS OF THE DARK SIDE

STAR WARS.

Book 4

MISSION from MOUNT YODA

PAUL DAVIDS
AND HOLLACE DAVIDS

Pencils by June Brigman
Finished Art by Karl Kesel

A BANTAM BOOK®
NEW YORK • TORONTO • LONDON • SYDNEY • AUCKLAND

MISSION FROM MOUNT YODA
A BANTAM BOOK 0 553 40530 6

First published in the USA by Bantam Skylark Books,
a division of Bantam Doubleday Dell Publishing Group, Inc.

First publication in Great Britain

PRINTING HISTORY
Bantam US edition published 1993
Bantam UK edition published 1993

Cover art by Drew Struzan
Interior pencils by June Brigman
Finished interior art by Karl Kesel

Bantam Books are published by Transworld Publishers Ltd,
61–63 Uxbridge Road, Ealing, London W5 5SA, in Australia by
Transworld Publishers (Australia) Pty Ltd, 15–25 Helles
Avenue, Moorebank, NSW 2170, and in New Zealand by
Transworld Publishers (NZ) Ltd, 3 William Pickering Drive,
Albany, Auckland.

Printed and bound in Great Britain by
Cox & Wyman Ltd, Reading, Berkshire

To Jeff Tinsley,
Your camera has always been your
lightsaber. May you continue to defend
and protect R2-D2 and C-3PO at their
home in the Smithsonian Museum of
American History.

Acknowledgments

With thanks to George Lucas, the creator of Star Wars,
to Lucy Wilson for her devoted guidance, to Charles
Kochman for his unfailing insight, and to West End
Games for their wonderful Star Wars sourcebooks—
also to Betsy Gould, Judy Gitenstein, Peter Miller,
and Richard A. Rosen for their advice and help.

The Rebel Alliance

Luke Skywalker

Princess Leia

Han Solo

Chewbacca

See-Threepio (C-3PO)

Artoo-Detoo (R2-D2)

Ken

Dustini

The Empire

Trioculus

Grand Moff Hissa

Supreme Prophet Kadann

High Prophet Jedgar

Zorba the Hutt

Defeen

Assassin Droid

Triclops

A long time ago,
in a galaxy
far, far away...

The Adventure Continues . . .

It was an era of darkness, a time when the evil Empire ruled the galaxy. Fear and terror spread across every planet and moon as the Empire tried to crush all who resisted—but still the Rebel Alliance survived.

The headquarters of the Alliance Senate are located in a cluster of ancient temples hidden within the rain forest on the fourth moon of Yavin. It was the Senate that now led the valiant fight to establish a new galactic government, and to restore freedom and justice to the galaxy. In pursuit of this quest, the Rebel Alliance leader, Mon Mothma, organized the Senate Planetary Intelligence Network, also known as SPIN.

SPIN conducts its perilous missions with the help of Luke Skywalker and his pair of droids known as See-Threepio (C-3PO) and Artoo-Detoo (R2-D2). Other members of SPIN include the beautiful Princess Leia; Han Solo, the dashing pilot of the spaceship *Millennium Falcon*; Han's copilot, Chewbacca, a hairy alien Wookiee; and Lando Calrissian, the former governor of Cloud City on the planet Bespin.

Lando Calrissian had been forced to abandon his post in Cloud City after gambling away his position to Zorba the Hutt, a sluglike alien who is the father of the deceased gangster, Jabba the Hutt. Having learned about his son's death at the hands of Princess Leia, Zorba now seeks revenge against Leia and the Rebel Alliance. Aided by the Force, Leia and her brother Luke, the last of the Jedi Knights, have managed to elude the wrath of the Hutt—at least for the time being.

The Jedi Knights, an ancient society of brave and noble warriors, believed that victory comes not just from physical strength but from a mysterious power called the Force. The Force lies hidden deep within all things. It has two sides, one side that can be used for good, the other side a power of absolute evil.

Guided by the Force, and by the spirit of his first Jedi teacher, Obi-Wan Kenobi, Luke Skywalker was led to the legendary Lost City of the Jedi. Deep underground on the fourth moon of Yavin, the Lost City proved to be the home of a boy named Ken, said to be a Jedi Prince. Ken had no human friends and had never before left the Lost City to journey above ground. He knew nothing of his origins and had been raised by a loyal group of caretaker droids who had served the ancient Jedi Knights. Ken has since left the underground city and joined Luke and the Rebel Alliance.

With the Empire's evil leaders, Emperor Palpatine and Darth Vader, now destroyed, a new era has begun. Kadann, the Supreme Prophet of the Dark Side, foretold that a new Emperor would arise, and on his hand he would wear an indestructible symbol of evil—the glove of Darth Vader! The prophecy was fulfilled when three-eyed Trioculus, the former Supreme Slavelord of Kessel, recovered the glove.

Upon taking command as leader of the Empire, Trioculus was warned by Kadann that he must first locate and destroy a certain Jedi Prince. This prince, Ken, had learned many dark and dangerous Imperial secrets from the droids of the Lost City. The information, if revealed, could threaten Trioculus's reign as Emperor, and bring it to a sudden and tragic end.

Trioculus failed in his mission, running up against Zorba the Hutt instead. Zorba imprisoned Trioculus in carbonite. He is now frozen in suspended animation, displayed in the Cloud City Museum as a living statue.

One of the more dangerous secrets known by Ken is that three-eyed Trioculus was an impostor who falsely claimed to be the son of Emperor Palpatine. Trioculus was aided in his rise to power by the grand moffs, in a plot they designed to share the rule of the Empire. The Emperor's real three-eyed son, Triclops, has been a prisoner in Imperial insane asylums for almost his entire life. For some mysterious reason the Empire fears him, still keeping him alive, while denying his very existence.

Luke Skywalker and his ragtag group of Rebel freedom fighters battled armor-clad stormtroopers and mile-long star destroyers. They have even exploded two of the Empire's mightiest weapons: the Imperial Death Stars, which were as big as moons and powerful enough to explode entire planets. Now this band of Alliance heroes has fled from Cloud City in the *Millennium Falcon* and departed for one of the most scenic planets in the galaxy—Z'trop. There, they are taking in some much needed rest before returning to Alliance headquarters.

Meanwhile, Kadann has summoned his loyal fellow Prophets of the Dark Side. They gather within his Chamber of Dark Visions in the cube-shaped Space Station Scardia, located somewhere deep in the Null Zone of space. Kadann's latest prophecies are about to bring forth a foreboding sense of doom for the Alliance, a threat that will give rise to a bold, new Alliance mission from a mountaintop on the planet Dagobah—a mission from Mount Yoda!

CHAPTER 1
Dark Prophecies

The men in glittering black robes marched single file down the long hallway inside Space Station Scardia.

It was a day of prophecy, a day when the mighty dwarf named Kadann, the Supreme Prophet of the Dark Side, would tell his fellow prophets what the future held in store.

High Prophet Jedgar, who was seven feet tall and towered above the other prophets, glanced out of the huge rectangular window inside the corridor. His thoughts were far away.

Peering into the emptiness of space, Jedgar tried to see beyond the Null Zone, to the star system of the planet Bespin. It was there that the official ruler of the Empire, three-eyed Trioculus, had been frozen alive inside a block of carbonite. Jedgar scowled, embarrassed by the disaster the Empire was experiencing. How could Trioculus have been so easily defeated and taken captive by the sluglike creature, Zorba the Hutt?

But if ever there was a man who knew how to turn disaster for the Empire to his own advantage, it was the aged and mysterious Kadann, Jedgar's evil master.

Slowly Jedgar and the other prophets approached the Chamber of Dark Visions, where Kadann was awaiting their arrival. As they walked through the huge doorway, Jedgar clutched the large black handwritten volume, *Secrets of the Dark Side*, that he held under his arm.

Facing a glowing red curtain, the prophets bowed, letting their beards touch the cold metal floor. Then they began to mumble a chant:

Dark power to Kadann and the Empire . . .
Dark power to Kadann and the Empire. . . .

The prophets then sat up and raised their eyes to watch as the red curtain in front of them slowly lifted. Behind the curtain sat Kadann, master of darkness and leader of a vast network of interplanetary spies. If Kadann's prophecies of the future ever failed to come true on their own, his spies would use any means possible, including blackmail and murder, to *make* them come true. In that way they assured that Kadann appeared incapable of ever making an error in his predictions.

Beside Kadann's chair rested a ball made of a black chalky substance. Kadann picked up the ball and crushed it in his hand, casting a dark powdery cloud throughout the chamber. Inhaling the chalky mist, High Prophet Jedgar was reminded that black was a symbol of victory for the Empire.

Kadann cleared his throat and began to speak.

As always when he prophesied, Kadann spoke in short verses that didn't rhyme—verses called quatrains—each one exactly four lines long.

> *Tormented and frozen alive*
> *The three-eyed ruler commands no more.*
> *Never again shall he receive*
> *The dark blessing of the Supreme Prophet.*

For a moment there was silence.

Then Jedgar spoke in a hoarse whisper. "Who then shall command the Empire now, Master?" he asked.

Kadann continued his prophecy:

> *Eyes cannot behold the new ruler,*
> *For the ruler is the Dark One of ancient times.*
> *But from this day forth he speaks through me,*
> *And I shall speak his commands to you.*

Using a laser pen, High Prophet Jedgar burned Kadann's words into a blank page in the book of secrets. Jedgar's heart pounded as he realized that, with those few words, Kadann had just declared himself to be the true spokesman for the source of all darkness in the galaxy.

Spellbound, Jedgar looked up from the book and gazed at Kadann. The Supreme Prophet of the Dark Side continued speaking, with eyes half-closed, as if in a deep trance:

Ancient relics of Duro shall you bring
To place at my feet and praise me.
In this chamber I will then destroy
All that is good in the Force.

Then Kadann's voice became so soft that every ear in the Chamber of Dark Visions had to strain to hear him:

When the Dragon Pack,
Perched upon Yoda's stony back,
Receives a visitor pierced by gold,
Then come the last days of the Rebel Alliance.

CHAPTER 2
The Dragon Pack on Yoda's Back

"I have a bad feeling about this," said Han Solo, as he and Princess Leia spotted a strange creature in the tidewater pool where they were swimming.

"Oh, Han, it's just a septapus," Princess Leia replied calmly, swimming over to Han. "They never hurt anybody."

Leia and Han, along with Luke Skywalker, Chewbacca, Ken, and their droids, were taking a vacation on the planet Z'trop, one of the most scenic planets in the galaxy. They were on a tropical, volcanic island, where the septapus, with its seven tentacles and five glowing eyes, had approached them in the shallow water along the bright blue shoreline. Now it was swimming away as fast as it could go.

"A septapus once picked a fight with me, and he lived to regret it," said Han. "They can get really nasty when they're hungry."

"That's unusual, Han," Leia said, raising an eyebrow skeptically. "I've always heard that the septapus is a gentle species. I've never known one to pick a fight with anyone."

"Tell that to the one that tried to eat me," Han shot back.

"Eat you?" Leia exclaimed in disbelief. "Han, they're vegetarians. They never eat anything but seaweed."

"Oh yeah?" Han challenged.

"Yeah," Leia insisted.

Han and Leia were due to report for a meeting on Mount Yoda, the secret Alliance base on the planet Dagobah. Han had hoped that he would have a chance first to share a few romantic days with Princess Leia. But somehow things weren't going as he had planned. He had a bad habit of turning every conversation with Leia into an argument. Han found it hard to believe that just a few days ago he had been seriously considering marriage.

He glanced toward the shore, where Luke Skywalker and Chewbacca were teaching Ken, the twelve-year-old Jedi Prince, a technique of self-defense.

Leia climbed out of the tidewater pool and walked over to the *Millennium Falcon*, which was parked on the beach nearby. Just then Artoo-Detoo, the barrel-shaped droid, rolled down the entrance ramp of the spaceship.

"*Tzzz-bnoooch! Bzeeeee-tzoooop!*" Artoo tooted.

See-Threepio, the golden droid, walked over from a grove of trileaf trees. He and the two other droids,

Chip and Kate, had been standing there in the shade to prevent their metal circuits from baking in the midday heat. "Oh dear, oh my," Threepio fretted. "Artoo says that he's detected an Imperial vehicle. Look, up on that bluff!"

"It's an Imperial Single Trooper Compact Assault Vehicle," said Luke, his eyes narrowing in the direction Threepio was pointing. "C'mon, Chewie. We'd better check this out."

"Hey, wait for me!" Ken exclaimed, as Luke and Chewbacca cautiously started up the trail that led to the top of the bluff.

"And me too!" shouted Han.

As they approached the Imperial vehicle, Luke noticed no sign of movement. The hatch behind the laser-cannon turret was wide open.

"Roooor-woooof," Chewbacca barked.

"You're right, Chewie," said Luke. "Nobody's here to operate it. Look, its treads have been split by the sharp volcanic rocks on this bluff."

"Maybe whoever was operating it deserted his post," Ken offered.

There was no laserfire, and they soon determined that the vehicle was indeed empty.

"A Compact Assault Vehicle doesn't necessarily signal the presence of an Imperial base," Luke explained. "It probably means just the opposite. The Empire uses these one-trooper vehicles on undeveloped worlds that aren't occupied territory. One trooper in a CAV can control a lot of territory."

Luke crawled inside, lowering himself through the hatch. Then he poked his head out. "I wonder if the missing Imperial trooper is dead," he mused. "Maybe he took a swim past the reefs and drowned in the rough current."

"Or maybe he was eaten by a septapus," Han Solo offered, having caught up with his companions on the bluff. "The type that isn't vegetarian."

Inspecting the interior of the well-armored combat vehicle, Luke found a small pouch filled with what seemed to be the personal possessions of an Imperial trooper: identification, a combat service medal, a personal hygiene kit, and a small gold knife. Luke also found several data discs. One of them was labeled with a triple "S."

Luke recognized the symbol immediately. "It stands for Space Station Scardia," he said with certainty.

"Scardia!" Ken exclaimed. He knew all about the space station from a master computer file in the library of the Lost City of the Jedi. "I wonder what kind of trouble Kadann and his Prophets of the Dark Side are up to now."

Luke and Han deactivated the vehicle's weapons; then they took the pouch and data discs with them as they headed back to Princess Leia and the droids. With the discovery of the Imperial Compact Assault Vehicle, their time for relaxing on the beach had come to an abrupt end.

Together they blasted off as Han piloted the *Millennium Falcon* into hyperspace.

Luke glanced over at Ken, who was sitting next to him in the spaceship's navigation room. The previous morning, Luke had broken the news to Ken that he would have to start going to school. That meant that very soon Ken would no longer be free to fly from planet to planet with Luke and the others, helping the Alliance. Luke could tell the Jedi Prince was depressed, because the boy was unusually quiet.

Luke turned his attention to the information on the captured data disc. He quickly discovered that the disc contained recent Imperial propaganda, dispatched from Space Station Scardia to the Imperial troops in the field. And the most significant propaganda, as far as Luke was concerned, was the list of the latest prophecies of Supreme Imperial Prophet Kadann.

"What does Kadann predict is going to happen to the Alliance in our war against the Empire?" Ken asked curiously, as he glimpsed the information on the data disc.

"No Imperial prophet has ever predicted that the Alliance would survive even *this* long," Luke explained, "so I certainly don't accept anything that Kadann has to say about the future. Besides, Yoda taught me that even though you may be able to glimpse the future through the Force, the future can change before it arrives. He said, 'Always in motion is the future.'"

"Still," Han commented, "lots of Imperials believe every word Kadann speaks— and some of them will do almost anything to try to *make* his prophecies come true. He can't be dismissed so easily."

Returning from lightspeed, the *Falcon* finally slowed and banked, soaring through Dagobah's misty atmosphere. Pilot Han Solo flew the spaceship toward the very peak of Mount Yoda, the highest point on the swamp-covered planet.

From afar, Luke could make out lights at the mountaintop. They were the lights from the Rebel Alliance military center—a metallic fortress with more than a dozen levels, and hundreds of beaming, glowing signals to guide friendly spacecraft through the ever-present clouds.

The fortress was DRAPAC, short for the Defense Research and Planetary Assistance Center. DRAPAC was also the site of Dagobah Tech, the Rebel Alliance school where Ken was about to begin classes.

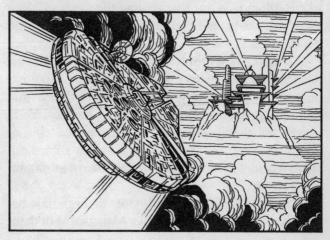

As the *Millennium Falcon* surged through the mist of Dagobah, Han Solo and his copilot, Chewbacca, steered an even course toward Mount Yoda's peak.

"How did Mount Yoda get its name, anyway?" Ken asked.

"We used to call it Mount Dagger," Luke explained, "but after Yoda died, it seemed appropriate to rename it in his memory, since this is the planet where he lived."

Luke sighed, feeling a lump in his throat. Every time he returned to Dagobah, memories of Yoda and the swamps where Yoda had trained him to become a Jedi Knight flashed through his mind.

Yoda may have been small in size, but he was mighty in wisdom. Although Luke felt that Yoda was always nearby in spirit, the galaxy was just not the same anymore without him.

The Millennium Falcon gently touched down on its docking bay. Moments later, the ragtag troop of the Alliance departed the spaceship.

"It's *so* good to be back among friends," said See-

Threepio, looking forward to a soothing oil and lube job. "Here at DRAPAC, a droid never has to worry about being taken apart by vicious Imperials and sold for scrap metal—or worse yet, melted down and made into gun barrels for Imperial ion cannons."

Ken looked around with wide-eyed wonder at everything Princess Leia showed him. She explained that the fortress was still not finished. The lower levels, buried deep inside Mount Yoda, were still being fitted with new laboratories.

According to Luke, the Alliance was pursuing its most top-secret project in one of those labs, safe from spies and the probe droids of the Empire. Its code name was Project Decoy.

The newly arrived members of the Rebel Alliance, as well as other members of SPIN, entered the banquet hall for a welcoming feast arranged by the Alliance leader, Mon Mothma. In the meantime, See-Threepio, Artoo-Detoo, Chip, and Kate went directly to the Droid Maintenance Shop to be oiled, lubricated, and polished.

SPIN, the Senate Planetary Intelligence Network, had until recently been based on Yavin Four, the jungle planet where the Lost City of the Jedi was located deep underground. However, Imperial attacks on the fourth moon of Yavin had caused Mon Mothma to select an alternate base to locate DRAPAC. The Empire had yet to mount a successful assault on the misty planet Dagobah, which was covered with marshes, bogs, swamps—and the steep and treacherous Mount Yoda.

Mon Mothma congratulated Luke Skywalker for returning with a data disc containing the latest prophecies of Kadann. Now they could study the prophecies at last.

Princess Leia read one of them aloud, as the assembled eagerly tried to interpret it.

When the dragon pack,
Perched upon Yoda's stony back,
Receives a visitor pierced by gold,
Then come the last days of the Rebel Alliance.

"When Kadann talks about Yoda's stony back, he must mean Mount Yoda," Leia offered.

"And I'm sure that the words 'dragon pack' refer to DRAPAC," Luke explained.

"What I don't understand," said Mon Mothma, "is what Kadann means when he talks about us receiving a visitor pierced by gold."

"Perhaps it has something to do with this," said Luke, opening the small pouch where he kept the data disc. "This contains a few personal possessions left behind by the missing Imperial pilot of the Compact Assault Vehicle."

Luke withdrew a small, sharp golden knife from the pouch. "I wonder if it's a warning that a visitor to DRAPAC is going to be pierced by this," he said, holding the knife up. Its golden blade gleamed in his blue eyes.

CHAPTER 3
The Scheme of the Grand Moffs

In Cloud City on the planet Bespin, the new Baron Administrator, Zorba the Hutt, slept restlessly.

In his fitful sleep the giant slug saw a vision of the deserts of Tatooine. And in his vision, amidst the swirling sands, he saw the empty, deserted palace that he had inherited from his son, Jabba.

In Zorba's dream, sharp-toothed Ranats were tearing the inside of the palace to shreds.

Suddenly the dream changed, as if Zorba was seeing the palace in the future. It had become a modern, interplanetary prison, an armed fortress where criminals from many different planets were sent for punishment and execution. Their deaths were fearsome—they were thrown into the Pit of Carkoon, where the Mouth of Sarlacc was buried in the sand, ready and eager to swallow its victims alive. The line of criminals stretched for miles, and for each one Zorba collected a fee.

Zorba awoke with a start, knowing at once that he would have to set to work immediately if he were to turn his dream into a profit-making reality. He was confident that the Cloud Police would keep order in Cloud City while he traveled to Tatooine.

However, only a few hours after Zorba's departure, Muskov, the Chief of the Cloud Police, sent a message to an Imperial strike cruiser that was orbiting high above Cloud City. The arrival of the Imperial spaceship was a signal that it was time for the chief to put into action the plan of the grand moffs, who wanted to rescue Trioculus from the Cloud City Museum and put him back on the throne of the Empire.

In the dark of night, a small, unmarked shuttle flew out of the strike cruiser and descended to Cloud City. Upon its arrival a small team of Imperial stormtroopers swiftly climbed out of the shuttle and proceeded to the back of a floating freight truck. When they arrived at the museum, the armed guards at the door allowed them to enter without incident.

The stormtroopers and Chief Muskov met by the wall where the body of Trioculus, encased in carbonite, was standing on display like a work of art. The stormtroopers paid the agreed-upon bribe. Then, silently and efficiently, the Imperial stormtroopers took the carbonite block and loaded it into the back of their floating freight truck.

Under cover of darkness, in a guarded hangar, they transferred the carbonite block to the inside of their shuttle. Then they blasted off, taking the carbonized body of their Imperial leader to Grand Moff

Hissa, who was awaiting their arrival inside the strike cruiser.

"Excellent!" said Grand Moff Hissa excitedly, as he beheld the carbonite block. Of all the grand moffs, Hissa was the one who had most devotedly schemed and plotted to put Slavelord Trioculus on the throne of the Empire. He gnashed his razor-sharp teeth gleefully as the carbonite block was presented to him in the master chamber of the strike cruiser. "At last we shall restore Trioculus! The moment draws near! Prepare to thaw out our Dark Lordship!" he proclaimed, pointing to the nearby flux-field generator, a device used for melting solid carbonite.

At that moment, however, the *Scardia Voyager*, the spaceship that belonged to the Prophets of the Dark Side, flew directly alongside the Imperial strike cruiser. It beamed a message to Grand Moff Hissa from High Prophet Jedgar. "Make arrangements for docking. We are sending a boarding party immediately to personally deliver a message from Supreme Prophet Kadann."

Grand Moff Hissa admitted the boarding party, knowing full well that no Imperial, from the ranks of grand moff all the way down to ranger sixth class, had ever refused a request from the Prophets of the Dark Side. And that was because the spies of Kadann were everywhere. And Kadann's spies permitted no insult or offense to go unnoticed for very long.

"I present to you an official order from Supreme

Prophet Kadann," High Prophet Jedgar began with a crafty smile. "You are to turn over the carbonite block containing the body of Trioculus to me."

"But my dear High Prophet Jedgar," Grand Moff Hissa protested, "the flux-field generator is already heated, ready to melt the carbonite and free Trioculus from his torment. Surely Kadann wouldn't wish our Emperor Trioculus to continue suffering in that horrid frozen state of suspended animation."

"Perhaps you've been inside the Moffship so long that you've lost touch with reality," High Prophet Jedgar said with a sneer. "Kadann no longer accepts Trioculus as our Emperor."

"But that is treason!" Grand Moff Hissa insisted, his face growing red with anger. "Kadann has never attempted to overthrow an Emperor before!"

"I must inform you," Jedgar continued with a snicker, "that there is no place whatsoever in Kadann's plans for Trioculus. Nor shall there be for you, unless you kneel at once and pledge your undying loyalty to Kadann as your only true leader!"

"My dear Jedgar, we have procedures to be followed in the Empire," Grand Moff Hissa replied, biting on the nail of his forefinger distractedly. "If Kadann feels that it's his duty to take command, then let him summon the Central Committee of Grand Moffs and ask us to agree to his—"

"Perhaps Kadann doesn't think as highly of the Central Committee of Grand Moffs as you do," High Prophet Jedgar interrupted, stroking his beard. "Perhaps you hasten the day when he'll decide that he no longer has a use for *any* grand moffs at all!"

"Perhaps *you* hasten the day," Grand Moff Hissa retorted, clenching his razor-sharp teeth, "when the Imperial grand moffs shall decide that we have no use for the Prophets of the Dark Side."

High Prophet Jedgar scowled, then his voice dropped to a hoarse whisper. "But before that day comes, Grand Moff Hissa," he said, "you would be arrested as a traitor. Perhaps you don't realize what damaging information Kadann has on you. Yours is the thickest file of all the grand moffs. I've brought you one page of it, so that you may reconsider your situation."

At that, Jedgar reached into his robe, withdrew a folded piece of paper, and handed it to Hissa.

As Hissa unfolded the page and read it, his eyes bulged and his breath quickened. Beads of sweat formed on his brow.

"How . . . how could he possibly know any of this?" Hissa stammered. "He can't prove a thing."

"We have witnesses, my dear Hissa," Jedgar said with a coy smile. "If Kadann reveals your file to the Imperial Security Forces, your execution is assured. You'll be thrown to a wild, raving Rancor beast to be eaten alive, or— "

"I deny these charges!" Grand Moff Hissa exclaimed. His eyes blinked rapidly, like the eyes of a trapped Ranat about to die.

"Deny it all you like. It will make no difference.

And you've only seen one page. Remember, your file is this thick," High Prophet Jedgar said, spreading his hands out about a foot apart.

His voice suddenly choked, and Grand Moff Hissa couldn't even reply.

"All this unpleasantness can be so easily avoided," Jedgar continued, baring his upper teeth as he sneered. "Just accept Kadann as leader of the Empire. Bend your right knee to the floor, and profess your loyalty to Kadann, your master until the end of time!"

Hissa's legs trembled. His right knee seemed to fall away beneath him, until it struck the cold metal floor.

"Kadann is my . . . master," Grand Moff Hissa said. "Until the . . . the end of time. . . ."

Jedgar scratched his bearded chin calmly. "*Very* good, my grand moff. Your pledge of loyalty to Kadann comes not a moment too soon. We have a job to do on the planet Duro. There has been a very unfortunate development there that concerns the Empire."

Hissa looked up at the figure of Jedgar towering above him. "As Kadann wishes. I accept my duty gratefully and with pleasure," Grand Moff Hissa said, grinding his teeth in disgust.

"Of course you shall," High Prophet Jedgar said, with a nod. "Now then, give the order to your stormtroopers, and let's settle the problem of the carbonite block once and for all."

Realizing he had no choice, Grand Moff Hissa gave the order. The carbonized body of Trioculus that the grand moffs had removed from the Cloud City Museum was then transported from the Moffship.

With regret Hissa watched as the carbonized block was taken to be stowed aboard the *Scardia Voyager*. He knew full well that it was a fateful moment—Hissa realized that the frozen body of Trioculus was on its way to Kadann, about to be destroyed aboard Space Station Scardia!

CHAPTER 4
The Golden Crown

"Do I *have* to start going to school like other kids?" Ken asked Luke. Together they walked with See-Threepio up the main hall of Dagobah Tech, to the room where Ken was scheduled to take a series of aptitude tests. Dagobah Tech was where all the sons and daughters of DRAPAC scientists studied.

"School is a great adventure and a real opportunity," Luke replied. "When I was only a few years older than you, I wanted more than anything else to study at the Academy. All my friends got to go—and I envied them. But from the time I was a kid, my Uncle Owen and Aunt Beru needed my help on their moisture farm."

"Well, I'd rather work on a moisture farm than go to school," Ken said.

"Moisture farms are hot and lonely," Luke insisted. "And besides, they're all on miserable desert worlds, like Tatooine. End of discussion. Period."

Ken groaned as he went off and took the aptitude tests, which covered every subject from spaceship repair to galactic history. The tests were harder than he'd expected. He breezed through the questions on advanced math concepts and droid microcircuits, but he was stumped by the parts on alien languages and space navigation.

Things went from bad to worse when he tackled the questions on exobiology, the study of alien life forms. A lot of the questions were about g'nooks, a species of rather unintelligent apelike humanoids with very small brains. The test was so dumb, Ken decided that only a g'nook could have designed it.

After Ken finished, Luke and See-Threepio were waiting right where they had said they would be—beneath the sign that said DAGOBAH TECH, outside the main office of the school.

Ken complained about the aptitude tests as he, Luke, and Threepio walked briskly up the rocky path that led from the Dagobah Tech Counseling Center to the DRAPAC dining hall.

All of a sudden a whining sound came from the sky.

VREEEEEK!!

A small cargo spaceship descended from high above, rumbling and vibrating, as if damaged. The descending craft sounded the interplanetary distress code.

Luke, Ken, and Threepio weren't the only ones to observe the spaceship. Two Y-wing fighters zoomed out of a DRAPAC hangar and flew alongside the damaged ship, escorting it to a landing pad.

The cargo ship wobbled as it descended, suddenly dropping to the ground far short of the Mount

Yoda hangars. Just before it was about to crash, it broke its fall with a blast from its anti-gravity thrusters, cushioning the landing.

Ken glanced at the spaceship in wonder, noticing strange, alien writing on the side of the disabled craft.

"That writing is a language called Durese," said Threepio, who was fluent in six million languages. "Apparently, this spaceship is called *The Royal Carriage*. It is from the planet Duro."

A porthole creaked open, and a tall, gray-skinned humanoid with narrow eyes, a wide mouth, and no nose stepped outside.

Luke instinctively drew his lightsaber, unsure of

what to expect. But then he lowered his weapon when the pilot of the ship raised his hands, signaling that he was unarmed.

Ken stared at the alien, scrutinizing his furrowed brow and hollow cheeks, his long arms and fingers, and his boots. The alien was breathing heavily, ready to collapse from exhaustion.

"*Ick-zhana-von-zeewee,*" said the alien, reaching out to balance himself against a boulder.

"*Ick-zhana-zoo-poobesh,*" Threepio replied, speaking in Durese. "*Ick-vee-brash Luke Skywalker eeg Ken vopen Jedi.*"

The alien from the planet Duro reached for a

microelectronic device on the utility belt of his zippered gray uniform. He placed the device on his neck, and it stuck there.

"I beg your pardon, Mr. Skywalker and Mr. Ken," the Duro alien said politely, the neck device translating the guttural sounds from his throat. "I am Dustini. If you could be so kind as to spare me some food and water, I could—"

And then the alien dropped to his knees and fainted.

Rumors quickly spread throughout DRAPAC—tales about the horrible fate of the people of Duro. At great risk Dustini made the perilous journey from his home planet to Mount Yoda so the truth could be known.

After Dustini had quenched his hunger and thirst, bathed, and rested, Princess Leia and Alliance leader Mon Mothma called a meeting in DRAPAC's north tower, the site of their largest conference room. Even Ken was granted permission to attend, as they all gathered to hear Dustini explain the purpose of his mission.

"For years, the Empire has been turning my planet into a dumping ground for hazardous wastes," Dustini began. "But still, my people of Duro survived, relocating ourselves onto orbiting space stations. Only the archaeologists of Duro remain behind to resist the Empire. We have a proud and rich history," Dustini explained, "with many archaeological monuments and treasures from Duro's Golden Age. Nearly every schoolchild on every civilized planet learns about our ancient history—that glorious time when my people were ruled by the great Queen Rana, our wise lawgiver.

"But now," Dustini continued, "not only has the Empire turned our planet into a garbage dump of toxic chemicals, but Imperials have begun to steal the heritage of Queen Rana. Stormtroopers are stealing all the relics from our past and sending them to Space Station Scardia in the Null Zone. The Empire's about to wipe out our culture—we are to be only servants of the Empire and follow orders, that is all. But by taking everything that reminds us of our past, they will force us to forget our heritage and who we really are as a people. Kadann is a greedy, ruthless collector of ancient treasures. He craves the relics of Queen Rana so much, nothing will stand in his way."

Luke glanced at Princess Leia, nodding in agreement. He had heard that Kadann's passion for ancient relics was out of control. The more treasures Kadann owned, the more he wanted.

"Please understand the peril we face," Dustini exclaimed as he continued his story, his gray face turning a shade of white. "None of the remaining Duro archaeologists on my planet are safe. The Empire arrests us on sight, forcing us to help them uncover more of our relics to steal for Kadann. And so we have all gone into hiding. I am one of a group of fifteen that remains hidden underground, storing and protecting our planet's ancient art, statues, scrolls, jewels, books, and relics."

Dustini unlatched a cargo box and showed everyone some samples of what he had managed to save: a transparent crystal in the shape of the face of Queen Rana, an ancient scroll of the wise laws of Rana, the rings of Rana, golden plates with picture-symbols from the dawn of civilization on Duro, and a golden crown from the days of King Dassid, Rana's son.

"Look," Dustini said, lifting the crown to his head, "this crown is just one of our many beautiful treasures."

VIIIIIIP!

"Ahhhhhh!" Dustini cried, grasping his head as his eyes turned upward.

Dustini toppled to the ground. He was paralyzed, his body locked in a twisted position, unable to bend or even stir. The translation microelectronic

device fell from his neck, as the crown tumbled from his head and rolled onto the floor.

"Zockkkk . . . izzzzh . . . tzzzzt . . ." Dustini stammered, but as hard as he tried, he could no longer speak. He took short, gasping breaths, staring blankly toward the ceiling of the conference room.

"Zaaaaahh . . . kiiiiii . . ."

"Oh my!" Threepio exclaimed. "It appears that the crown was a booby trap, designed to kill any thief who plundered King Dassid's tomb."

Luke kneeled beside Dustini, lifting the crown to examine it. He spied several tiny holes and needles inside; they must have pierced Dustini's head, he thought. "Threepio, quick!" Luke said. "Summon the medical droids at once!"

The medical droids arrived swiftly, bringing with them a cart to move Dustini to the medical center for examination and treatment. But as the medical droids leaned over to lift him, Dustini struggled, trying to move his paralyzed limbs. "Zoooock . . . izzzzh . . ."

Dustini managed to wiggle a finger. The finger trembled as he pointed it toward the jacket of his gray uniform. "Zaaaahh . . ."

"His pocket!" See-Threepio exclaimed. The golden droid inspected Dustini's upper pocket. Inside, Threepio found a small hologram disc, which he promptly handed over to Luke for inspection.

The medical droids then removed Dustini from the conference room.

"Artoo," said Luke, "let's see if this hologram

disc fits into your projection slot. It seems to be the right format."

The little barrel-shaped droid rolled toward Luke on its three metal legs. "*Dwee boopa-ooonnn*," he whistled as Luke attempted to put the data disc into the correct slot.

"It seems that Kadann's prophecy is starting to come true already," said Mon Mothma, her brow knitted in deep concern.

"You're right," Leia agreed. "Dustini must be the visitor to Mount Yoda who Kadann predicted would be pierced by gold. It had nothing to do with the golden knife Luke found on Z'trop after all. However, Kadann predicted that the last days of the Alliance would begin now."

"Well then," Luke said with determination, "we'll just have to prove that black-bearded dwarf dead wrong."

Artoo-Detoo spun his domed top left and right excitedly. "*Bdeee-zhiiip!*" he beeped. Seconds later a bright light inside Artoo projected a hologram of Dustini's face. It seemed to float in the middle of the room.

"*Zki-mip-conosco-zhoren*," the hologram began.

Threepio began to translate the message at once. "Dustini says that he made this holographic recording so that if anything happened to him, his urgent mission on behalf of the archaeologists of Duro would not end in failure, and the Alliance leaders here on Mount Yoda would still receive his message."

"*Khiz-ipm-ikzee-zeldar,*" the hologram of Dustini continued.

"Dustini requests that we fly on a mission from Mount Yoda to Duro," Threepio explained, "to save Dustini's fellow archaeologists and prevent the ancient treasures of Duro from being stolen by Kadann."

"*Zhik-meez-bzooop.*"

"There's more information on the disc, but there seems to be a glitch. Artoo can't tell us any more."

CHAPTER 5
Destination Duro

Ken awoke the next morning with a churning feeling in his stomach. Luke, Leia, Han, Chewbacca, and the droids were going off to Duro without him, and Ken was being left behind to attend classes at Dagobah Tech. Ken was feeling upset. Why did he have to go to school, anyway? He could learn everything he needed to know while going off on Alliance missions.

"Hurry, hurry," said Chip, Ken's personal droid. He was standing beside Ken's bed. "Get up. Up-up-up. You have to get dressed, wash your face, brush your teeth, comb your hair, and zip downstairs to the commissary to have breakfast. Quickly now—and find your computer notebook. Do you remember where you put it?"

"Okay, Chip, I'm getting up," Ken said.

Chip certainly is bright-eyed and on his toes for such an early hour of the morning, Ken thought. But then again, droids never had the unpleasant experience of having to wake up from a deep sleep. At all hours of the day and night, droids always remained alert, fully charged, and ready to go.

Ken glanced at the timepiece beside his bed, in

the comfortable cubicle he had been assigned to live in at DRAPAC. "I'm skipping breakfast today," he insisted. "I want to say good-bye to Luke and everybody before they blast off for Duro. They haven't left yet, have they?"

"They're probably in the hangar, boarding," Chip replied. "You'd better make it a quick good-bye. You won't make a good impression on anyone if you're late for the first day of school!"

Ken washed, dressed, brushed his teeth, and combed his hair; then he hurried outside the main DRAPAC building, running all the way to the hangar where the *Millennium Falcon* was docked on a landing pad.

"Luke, Leia, are you there?" Ken called out, peering through the open hangar door. He blinked, as the hangar's overhead illuminators glared in his eyes. "I just came by to say good-bye and wish you a—"

Ken fell silent, suddenly realizing that no one was inside the hangar to hear him. "Anybody here?" he shouted again, but all he heard was the echo of his own voice. There was no sign of any humans or other biological life-forms in the hangar—not even any droids.

Maybe they were already on board, making last-minute preparations.

Ken walked inside the hangar to see if Luke or any of the others were inside the spaceship. He popped through the hatch and air lock, but was disappointed to discover that no one else was on board. Maybe they were back in the cargo bay of the *Millennium Falcon*, near the engineering station and service access. They were probably strapping down their gear to get ready for takeoff.

Ken went back to check. When he entered the cargo bay, he discovered that all of the supplies for the journey to Duro had already been packed and strapped, and no one was—

CHHH . . . CHHH . . . CHHH.

Ken thought he heard the sound of boots walking near the quadrex power core. He swung around to look, accidentally knocking into a loose transport crate and sending it toppling against the cargo door's emergency control mechanism.

CRASH!

Suddenly the bulkhead door to the cargo bay swung shut.

FWOOOOOP! CLIIIICK!

It was locked!

Ken gulped. In the dull light of the cargo bay he surveyed the damage to the device that controlled the door. It was broken. And not only was the door mechanism damaged, but a cable attached to the wall was also sliced.

Ken pounded on the door. He tried to pry it open, but he had no luck. His heart sank.

"Help!" he shouted. "Can anybody hear me? I'm locked in the cargo bay!"

The bulkhead door was very thick. Ken suspected that even if Luke, Han, Leia, Chewbacca, and

the droids were now aboard, they wouldn't be able to hear him. Even Artoo-Detoo's sound sensors probably wouldn't be able to detect him back here.

Ken tried pushing on the door one more time, then gave up, collapsing to the floor in despair.

"Help, let me out of here, I'm supposed to start school!" he shouted.

Ken sat there, desperately trying to think of some way to escape. Then the soft white light turned red, and the entire hold rumbled with the sudden sound of the ship's power converter and ion flux stabilizer.

The rumbling increased, and Ken was slammed against the floor of the cargo hold, pressed down by an incredibly strong pressure. Unless he was mistaken, he was now on his way to the planet Duro!

With full obedience to the will of Kadann and High Prophet Jedgar, Grand Moff Hissa was also en route to Duro. But Hissa had no clue as to the purpose of his voyage. Now that Kadann had seized control of the Empire, the grand moffs no longer had access to the highest levels of top-secret information.

Hissa's strike cruiser encountered no space traffic along the way, no sign of any Imperial starfighters, no TIE fighters, or even any probe droids. However, as the gray and dying world of Duro came into view, Hissa spied a spacecraft that had a shape he recognized instantly—the *Millennium Falcon*!

"Opportunity strikes, Jedgar!" Hissa exclaimed. "That's Han Solo's spaceship up ahead. If fortune is with us, then Solo will have some important passengers aboard. And I'm not speaking of that oaf-brained Wookiee he calls his copilot. The reward on Chewbacca's head is only ten thousand credits. But if Luke Skywalker and Princess Leia are flying with him—"

"Call your best sharpshooters to the forward ion cannons!" High Prophet Jedgar commanded.

"Right away," Grand Moff Hissa snapped with a salute.

"And I have a splendid idea," Jedgar continued, stroking his beard thoughtfully. "This will be a contest to determine the best gunner aboard. Whoever destroys the *Millennium Falcon* shall have the pleasure of dining with Kadann and me aboard Space Station Scardia!"

Four Imperial gunners who were skilled weapons masters immediately took up positions at the forward ion cannons. Trained to handle everything from single-light laser cannons to turbolaser units, the gunners blasted the *Falcon* at full power.

Round after round was targeted at the main power thrusters, as Han Solo's ship weaved in and out to avoid the laserfire.

Then the *Falcon* turned to face the Imperial strike cruiser. Han returned the fire, but his ship's quad laser cannons were incredibly weak.

Grand Moff Hissa laughed. "If that's the best the Rebel Alliance can do in their defense, they'd be wise to surrender and plead for their lives," he scoffed.

* * *

Aboard the *Millennium Falcon* Han Solo was surprised by the weak firepower of his spaceship.

"I only want to know one thing," Han said in disgust. "Who was the Kowakian lizard-monkey who fooled around with our quad laser cannons and busted them?" Frowning, Han pounded a fist on the air lock beside him in frustration. "I had a full systems checkup at DRAPAC before we left Mount Yoda, and everything was purring like a mooka!"

"Artoo," Luke said, turning to his little barrel-shaped droid. "Find out if the problem is in our anticoncussion field generator, or whether something's wrong with the torplex deflector cable."

A thin rod popped out of Artoo-Detoo and plugged itself into the *Falcon's* master sensor unit. "*Kzeeep Kvoooch-Bzeeek*!" Artoo beeped.

"Artoo has located the problem, Master Luke," See-Threepio explained, waving his arms frantically toward the engineering station at the rear of the spaceship. "There's trouble with a power cable back in the cargo bay, near the bulkhead door that connects with the service access area. In fact, Artoo says that the cargo-bay door is jammed shut. Not only that, but the hyperdrive modulator appears to be loose. Oh my! We've no chance of escaping if we can't go into hyperdrive!"

"Can he unfreeze the bulkhead door so we can get inside the cargo bay and repair the damage?" Princess Leia asked, keeping an eye on the laserfire coming from the Imperial strike cruiser.

"Graaaawg!" Chewbacca interrupted, as the navigation control panel of the *Millennium Falcon* began vibrating beneath his furry hands.

The attack from the Imperial guns was getting worse. Han Solo had to keep the *Falcon* spinning in order to dodge the blasts. But he couldn't keep it up for much longer.

"*Chzootch Gneek!*" Artoo buzzed, turning his dome back and forth quickly.

"I'm afraid the outlook is very discouraging, Master Luke," Threepio explained. "The bulkhead door controls have been smashed."

"There must be a way to unfreeze that door," Luke insisted, getting up quickly and heading for the cargo bay.

"Master Luke, wait for me!" Threepio shouted, as he hurried alongside to assist. Artoo rolled along with them as well.

When they reached the bulkhead door, Luke heard a strange sound.

THUMP! THUMP! THUMP!

"Someone's pounding on the other side of the door," Luke said. "We've got a stowaway! Maybe our quad cannons and hyperdrive modulator were sabotaged by an Imperial spy!"

SCREEECH!

Suddenly the *Millennium Falcon* rumbled as it took a direct hit from Imperial fire. Threepio braced himself, but Luke toppled to the floor, as Artoo rolled forward, slamming into the door.

"Master Luke, get up!" Threepio screamed, but Luke remained on the floor, sitting upright with his eyes closed. "Master Luke, are you alright?"

"Quiet, Threepio," Luke explained. "Can't you see I'm concentrating on the Force?"

Luke tried to calm himself, using a Jedi mind technique to focus his thoughts on the door's latch. Emptying his mind of all thoughts, he allowed the great universal power of the Force to flow through him.

Luke then opened his eyes and aimed his gaze at the lock to the bulkhead door.

TZIP! KNIK!

The lock tumblers came free! The latch of the lock was moving!

FWOOOOP!

The bulkhead door began to rise!

Luke jumped to his feet and drew his lightsaber blade to confront the Imperial spy on the other side of the door.

Seeing the dark silhouette in front of him, Luke began to swing his blade at the saboteur. Then Luke gasped, pulling his blade aside at the last instant. It wasn't a spy after all! It was Ken, who was rushing frantically through the bulkhead doorway toward Luke!

"Way to go, Luke!" Ken shouted. "You saved my life!"

Luke shook his head, unable to believe his eyes.

"Saved you? I nearly destroyed you with my lightsaber! What are you *doing* here, Ken? You're supposed to be back at Mount Yoda starting school today!"

"I'm sorry, Luke. It was an accident."

"Some accident!" Luke snapped. "You hid aboard our ship so you wouldn't have to go to school. It's your first day, and already you're playing hooky!"

"No, Luke, that wasn't what happened, honest," Ken pleaded. "I thought you and the others had already boarded the *Millennium Falcon*, and I came to say good-bye and wish you a safe journey. When I called out and you didn't answer, I looked around. The next thing I knew—"

"The next thing you knew, you'd practically destroyed our quad laser cannons and smashed the control to the bulkhead door," Luke said, "*and* shut down our hyperdrive. Now we can't escape!"

"But it wasn't my fault," Ken protested. "There was a loose crate and—"

Luke, Ken, and Threepio quickly braced themselves, as more Imperial laserfire hit the *Millennium Falcon*—probably at the intake vent for the ship's cooling system. Artoo fell over onto his back, his dome striking the hard metal floor. "I'll help you, Artoo," Ken said, lifting the barrel-shaped droid back up. "Somebody should have manufactured you with hands, little droid. Then you wouldn't have these problems."

"*Bzeeebch bzooop!*" Artoo tooted in gratitude.

"Success!" Threepio shouted, unaware of Artoo and his troubles. "I've just replaced this piece of torn cable. Our quad laser cannons should be working splendidly now! By tightening up the connector to the hyperdrive modulator, I seem to have fixed it!"

The *Millennium Falcon's* defensive guns climbed up to full power again. And the lights on the display panel indicated to Han and Chewbacca that they could now use the hyperdrive and accelerate to light speed once again.

"Nice move!" Han said, as Luke returned to the navigation room. "Hey, what's the kid doing here?" he asked upon seeing the young Jedi Prince tagging along behind Luke.

"Ken!" Princess Leia exclaimed, shocked to see the boy aboard.

But Leia was even more shocked when, instead

of going into hyperdrive and escaping at faster-than-light speed, Han Solo began playing a dangerous game of space-tag. The *Falcon* darted toward Grand Moff Hissa's Imperial strike cruiser, as Han and Chewbacca took aim.

"Not so close, Han," Princess Leia shouted. "If they're going to blow up the *Falcon*, don't make it any easier for them!"

"Nobody's going to blow us up, Princess," Han said confidently. "We're just going to puncture a few holes in their air locks so those cocky Imperials can say good-bye to their air. Then they can eat our space dust!"

But Han had spoken too soon.

Grand Moff Hissa's marksmen made a direct hit on the *Millennium Falcon's* backup cooling system. And then, to add insult to injury, they melted the *Falcon's* missile tubes.

Han and Chewbacca had no choice but to cut the battle short, shift their spaceship into hyperdrive, and run from the fight at faster-than-light speed.

CHAPTER 6
Near the Valley of Royalty

In the Null Zone of space, deep inside Space Station Scardia, a group of Prophets of the Dark Side gathered around the carbonite block that had just been delivered.

The carbonite was now on a thick platform, directly below the deadly neutron furnace that powered the cube-shaped space station. Trioculus's face stuck out of the block, covered with a thick film of carbonite, looking as though he had been sculpted in black marble.

Kadann had given Trioculus his dark blessing to rule the Empire. With help from Grand Moff Hissa, Trioculus had fulfilled Kadann's prophecy about the new Imperial leader:

After Palpatine's fiery death
Another leader soon comes to command the Empire
And on his right hand he does wear
The glove of Darth Vader!

Kadann gazed deeply at the frozen face of Trioculus. It was no longer the face of the confident and brash liar who had once visited Kadann to prove that he wore the indestructible symbol of Imperial might—the right-hand glove of Darth Vader. It was now a twisted, burned, and tormented face—the face of a failure who had never measured up to his dark mission, and a disgrace to the Empire. Trioculus had failed to locate the Lost City of the Jedi—or the young Jedi Prince who was raised in the Lost City by Jedi caretaker droids.

Kadann sneered, knowing that the fateful end of Trioculus was close at hand.

Kadann hobbled over to the trigger that was to blast the carbonite block with deadly rays from the neutron furnace. The black-bearded dwarf shook his head in disgust, then touched the trigger.

TZZZZZZZZZZCH!

The scorching heat of four fiery neutron beams struck the carbonite block from all sides. The carbonite blistered, buckled, turned white-hot, and then, as the Prophets of the Dark Side shielded their eyes from the blast of intense light, the block completely vaporized.

When Kadann released his fingertip from the trigger of the neutron beam, there was nothing left of the block at all. Not even a trace of it remained on the platform.

Kadann turned to Prophet Gornash, the massive prophet who towered alongside him.

"It's done," Kadann declared.

"But the glove," Prophet Gornash objected. "The

glove of Darth Vader is indestructible. Why isn't the glove still on the platform?"

Kadann's smile didn't fade. "You call yourself a prophet, Gornash, and yet you cannot answer such an obvious question?"

"Regretfully, Kadann, the answer truly eludes me," Gornash replied, raising his brows quizzically. "Unless, perhaps, we have just vaporized someone else, not Trioculus."

"But for that to be the case, I would have to be mistaken," Kadann said. "And in this universe, Gornash, all things are possible, except one. And what may that one thing be? Say it, prove that I have taught you well."

"It's impossible that you could ever be mistaken, all-seeing, all-knowing Supreme Prophet of the Dark Side!" Gornash replied, bravely glancing at the stern face of Kadann.

Kadann nodded slowly. "You are correct. Have no doubt that Trioculus has been destroyed. But the glove—the glove still exists. In fact, the day Trioculus removed it, it was already on its way to me here, thanks to the efficient work of High Prophet Jedgar and my secret team of Imperial intelligence agents."

Kadann unlocked one of his thousands of display cases in Space Station Scardia and removed a delicately carved black box made of onyx. He lifted the lid and revealed the glove of Darth Vader! "Behold!" Kadann declared triumphantly. "No greater symbol of darkness was ever made than this glove—

the gauntlet that once covered Darth Vader's right hand. When it caused Trioculus to go blind because of his unworthiness, he removed it and began to wear a replica of the glove—one that was a fake, just like Trioculus himself. And now that he's been vaporized, may that liar and impostor never rest in peace!"

The *Millennium Falcon* came out of hyperdrive and circled back toward the planet Duro, zigzagging its way as it approached one of the six huge shipyards orbiting the gray planet. The *Falcon* was almost out of control.

FZZZZ—SWOOOOOSH!

The cooling system was leaking fluid into the cargo bay, causing a small flood.

KABUM . . . KABUM . . . KABUM . . .

And the *Falcon's* melted missile tubes rattled against one another, weakening their bearings.

"This ship is in sorry shape," Princess Leia lamented, as Han Solo slowed the spacecraft to approach a shipyard docking bay.

"No need to despair, Princess," Han replied. "The Duro mechanics at these shipyards are the best in the galaxy. They'll have the *Falcon* repaired in no time."

"Growwwrrr-rooowf!" Chewbacca barked.

"I'm afraid you're right, Chewie," Han said. "They'll have it repaired *if* they have the spare parts we need. If not, we could be laid up for weeks."

Despite the flood in the cargo bay, Han and Chewbacca managed to navigate the spaceship to Orbiting Shipyard Alpha—a shipyard circling Duro in a wide, oval orbit about a hundred miles above the planet's atmosphere.

A Duro mechanic at the shipyard quickly looked the *Millennium Falcon* over and told Han what the estimated bill would be for repairing it. All Han could say was, "Ouch!"

The Imperial attack from Grand Moff Hissa's strike cruiser had done more damage than anyone aboard the *Falcon* had expected. The replacement list included a brand new passive sensor antenna, a re-built Carbanti 29L electromagnetic package, a new acceleration compensator, extensive repairs to the ion flux stabilizer, and even a new floor for the flood-damaged cargo bay.

"A lot of bad news for one day, Han," Luke said, as Han paced back and forth nervously. "The *Millennium Falcon* is like a member of your family."

"Tell me about it," Han said with dismay.

"It's all my fault," Ken said.

"Owwwwwooooooooo!" Chewbacca howled, moaning as if he'd just stepped on a thick avabush thorn. But it was a moan of sorrow, not pain.

The shipyard sent a sales representative to talk to Han about the situation.

"The bottom line here, Mr. Solo," said the salesman, "is that it'll be less expensive to scrap the *Millennium Falcon* and buy a new spaceship, than it would be to repair it. Now this shipyard can offer you a trade-in on a new model Carbanti DeLuxe with a supercharged hyperdrive unit. Or we could even give you a great deal on a Novaldex Space Warper, with six months guarantee in the case of any Imperial attacks. It's up to you!"

Han suddenly got a splitting headache. "No deal," he said. "I want my *Falcon* back in one piece. She might be just a hunk of tin to you, but the *Millennium Falcon* means as much to me as Luke's droids here mean to him. You don't think Luke would trash See-Threepio and Artoo-Detoo just because they've got a few scratches and dents on them, do you?"

"You tell him, sir!" See-Threepio added, turning to the salesman. "We aren't interested in your new spaceships, and that's final!"

"I'm sure Mon Mothma will agree that the Alliance should pick up the tab for the repairs, Han," Leia said confidently. "After all, we made this flight at SPIN's request."

"Fix it," Han declared to the salesman.

While the *Millennium Falcon* was raised up on a huge rack in the repair bay, Princess Leia and Han Solo went to the rental agency in another warehouse in Shipyard Alpha and leased a Corellian Action VI Transport, so they could continue their mission.

As soon as the lease papers were signed, they blasted off from the orbiting shipyard and headed toward Duro. Luke, Leia, and Ken sat in the second tier of seats behind Han and Chewbacca in the navigation console, with Threepio and Artoo beside them.

"No wonder almost all the aliens on Duro got passports to live on other worlds," Princess Leia said, staring through the window down at the pockmarked gray planet. "There must be thousands of hazardous waste pits and toxic chemical landfills down there."

"*Tzzzn-gleEEEch chbziiit-tlooog!*" beeped Artoo-Detoo. The barrel-shaped droid suddenly projected a map.

"Look, Master Luke," Threepio said.

"Artoo must have fixed the glitch in Dustini's data disc," Princess Leia explained. "He's showing us the rest of the information."

The map showed a valley surrounded by a thick wall, with mountains beyond. The sound of Dustini's voice came from the data disc.

"We're seeing a schematic drawing of the Valley of Royalty on Duro," Threepio translated. "The wall has prevented unwelcome creatures from entering the valley for thousands of years. Now we're seeing beneath the valley, underground—ancient catacombs, caverns, and tunnels—all secret and unknown to the Empire."

The hologram then changed to an image of a Duro spaceship landing in the mountains near the valley. The spaceship touched down in a concealed flat region beneath the shelter of overhanging cliffs. Suddenly, a small part of the mountain glowed red.

"The red area is a hidden doorway," Threepio continued. "It's an entrance that leads down into the mountain—a tunnel beneath the wall that surrounds the Valley of Royalty. It leads to the caverns where the Duro archaeologists are hiding while they gather the treasures of their planet."

All eyes in the spacecraft continued to stare at the hologram, as the view changed once again. This time a building was revealed in the Valley of Royalty, not far from some ancient monuments. "That's the new Imperial Reprogramming Institute," Threepio said, "where the Empire sends its most dangerous prisoners."

Just then the hologram soundtrack stuck, repeating the following words in Durese: "*Ghinish-vik-Triclops . . . Ghinish-vik-Triclops . . .*"

"That building is where the Empire is keeping Triclops prisoner," Threepio explained.

"Don't you mean *Trioculus*?" Princess Leia asked, knitting her brows.

"No, he definitely said *Triclops*," Threepio replied.

"Well, who is Triclops?" Luke asked.

"I know," said Ken. "I probably should have told

you sooner, Luke, but Dee-Jay, my caretaker droid, said it would be dangerous to talk about Triclops to anyone—even to you. Triclops is the deepest, darkest secret of the Empire. The only Imperials who know of his existence are the most powerful members of the Imperial ruling class, such as the grand moffs."

"Then how do *you* know he exists, Ken?" a very puzzled Princess Leia asked.

"From the master computer files in the Jedi Library—in the Lost City of the Jedi. I was never allowed to see the whole file on Triclops," Ken explained, "but from what I did see, I learned that Triclops, like his name implies, has three eyes, just like Trioculus. And it is *Triclops*, not Trioculus, who is the real son of the evil Emperor who used to rule the galaxy with Darth Vader—Emperor Palpatine."

Ken told all he knew, as everyone listened to him with undivided attention. "The grand moffs refuse to admit officially that Triclops exists. They believe he's insane, and they're terrified that if he's ever set free, he might take over as ruler of the Empire, and destroy everything in the galaxy, including them! And yet, despite this danger, for some strange reason I don't understand, they still keep him alive!"

Under heavy cloud cover, the Corellian Action VI Transport began to descend.

"Thank your lucky stars that this freighter is a Corellian ship," Han said with satisfaction. "When I noticed this big brown knob over here on the master control board, it clinched the rental deal for me. Know what this doohickey does?"

"Is that for bailing out if we're going to crash?" Luke asked with a smile.

"I know what it's for," Ken said, his eyes bright and alert. "It's a Forbes CC-Y Antiradar Defense Unit."

"Bright kid," Han said with a sigh, shaking his head. "Did you also pick that up at the Jedi Library in the Lost City?"

"Of course," Ken replied. "Dee-Jay taught a special class in stealth systems."

Han pushed on the brown knob as he guided the Action VI Transport down toward the mountains. "I'm sure Dee-Jay probably taught you that this CC-Y unit makes us invisible to Imperial radar," Han continued. "Without it we'd look as big as a star dragon on enemy radar screens."

As they came in for their landing, the belly of the Corellian Transport scraped against the mountain ridge. *WHOOOOOSH—SHHHHHH.*

Clouds of hot exhaust gases billowed out of the transport's hyperdrive multiplier as it shut down.

Ken poked his head out of the transport ship's door and took two steps down the exit ramp. Through the gray mist he could see the outline of the Great Wall far below. He also saw a huge dam looming above the valley, bubbling with foul-smelling toxic wastes from Imperial spaceship manufacturing plants.

"That must be the Valley of Royalty down there!" Ken said excitedly. "Let's get going!"

"Wait a second," Luke said, coming down the ramp. "Where do you think *you're* going, Ken?"

"With you guys, of course. To save the archaeologists!"

Luke shook his head. "I'm assigning you to stay behind with Artoo and Chewie on board the ship. Leia, Han, See-Threepio, and I are going to head under the wall. This mission could prove far too dangerous for you at your age."

Ken folded his arms and pouted. "At my age? But Luke, you weren't that much older than I am when you first joined the Alliance. Besides, what about all the stuff I know? *You* thought the brown knob on this Corellian Action VI Transport was for bailing out! *I'm* the one who knew that it was a Forbes CC-Y Antiradar Defense Unit!"

"That's exactly why you're staying behind, to

help Chewie take care of the spaceship," Luke said. "You know its whole layout. You know how to operate ground defense in case of an attack."

"Chewie knows all that stuff too, and so does Artoo-Detoo," Ken argued. "Luke, don't forget your dream of Obi-Wan Kenobi. He told you our destinies are linked together. What do you think he would say if he knew you were leaving me behind?"

Luke sighed in frustration.

What was a Jedi Knight to do with a kid like Ken? He never took no for an answer. No matter what the situation, Ken always knew the right thing to say to get under Luke's skin and make him do what Ken wanted.

"If it's all the same with you, Master Luke, I'd be more than happy to stay behind," Threepio interjected. "After all, you did say it would be dangerous."

"Don't *you* start," Luke silenced the droid. "We need you with us."

"I'll stay behind," Princess Leia announced. "I can help Chewie fly this freighter out of here if the Imperials spot us. Before I became a diplomat from Alderaan, part of my training was in flying Corellian Action VI Transports for mercy missions." Leia removed the emergency supply backpack she had just put on. "Here, Ken," she said, handing him the backpack. "If you're going to go through the tunnels and under the Great Wall with Luke and Han and Threepio, something tells me you're going to need this."

CHAPTER 7
The Search for the Secret Cavern

Grand Moff Hissa's Imperial strike cruiser, with High Prophet Jedgar on board, landed on Duro, on the hill at the other side of the Valley of Royalty. The spacecraft docked at the Imperial Toxic Waste Processing Plant, which was spewing clouds of black ash, creating an overcast, dreary gray sky.

Duro was filled with valuable metals needed for building starships. The Empire mined the metals, then pumped the deadly liquid toxins that remained into a vast lake, held back by an enormous dam.

High Prophet Jedgar and Grand Moff Hissa walked slowly along the edge of the dam. Then Jedgar turned to Hissa, saying, "Now that we are here, I can reveal to you the purpose of this mission. We have come . . . to recapture Triclops."

"Triclops—the son of Emperor Palpatine!" Grand Moff Hissa gasped. "He's escaped?"

"Unfortunately, yes," Jedgar replied. "But not for long. He was a patient in our Imperial Reprogramming Institute, down there—"

Staring down at the sweeping valley, Grand Moff Hissa's eyes were blinded by bright gleams of silver.

Hissa could see the reflections from the flat, one-story Imperial Reprogramming Institute, near the Monument of Duchess Geneer, a tall dome with four spires. There was a silvery glint from King Kadlo Tower, the tallest structure—and also a gleam from the Monument to Queen Rana, a giant likeness of the ancient queen's face, which looked up to the sky.

"The search for Triclops is already underway," High Prophet Jedgar explained. He pointed to the swarms of stormtroopers fanning out from the Reprogramming Institute to look for the escaped prisoner. "Triclops escaped from Experimental Section Two, where even the most insane prisoners eventually learn obedience and to accept the rule of the Empire."

"Is Defeen, the Defel alien, still in charge of Experimental Section Two?" the grand moff asked. "If so, then he should be held accountable."

"Defeen was promoted to the position of interrogator first class," Jedgar replied. "In fact, Defeen traced the responsibility for the escape to a defective Imperial assassin droid who aided and abetted Triclops."

Looking down at the Great Wall, Grand Moff Hissa realized that without a spaceship, cloud car, or airspeeder, there was no way that Triclops could have gotten over the wall to flee from the Valley of Royalty. Triclops had to be down there—somewhere.

* * *

Luke, Han, Threepio, and Ken walked cautiously through a narrow, rocky gorge, searching for the hidden stairwell to the Valley of Royalty. Looking up at a craggy ledge, Luke spotted a giant Fefze beetle. No sooner did he point it out to the others than Threepio spotted several more coming up the gorge behind them.

"Oh my, I, I . . . I absolutely *deplore* giant insects of any kind!" Threepio stammered. "Especially beetles twice my size!"

"Look out—in front of us!" Ken shouted.

They were trapped! Four more giant Fefze beetles came scurrying toward them from farther away, at the front of the gorge. The beetles' antennas waved back and forth as each of their shiny bodies scampered along on six hairy legs.

"*AGAAAAA . . . AGAAAAA . . . .*" the Fefze beetles hissed.

"That must be the sound those buggers make when they're starving and smell food," Han said, firing his laserblaster at the ones that were behind them.

Han aimed at the giant insects' heads.

ZAAAAP!

Green fluid poured out of their beelike eyes, and then, as the beetles reared up, Han blasted their soft underbellies.

Luke pulled out his lightsaber and extended the bright green blade, as the Fefze beetles in front of them lined up one behind the other, charging through

the tight, narrow canyon.

CHOPPPPPP!

Luke sliced off the head of the first beetle as it attacked. The next one climbed up on the body of the dead insect, using it as a springboard to leap at Ken.

"Ken, duck!" Luke shouted.

WHOOOOOOSH!

Luke's sizzling lightsaber blade whacked the second giant insect in half, the pieces narrowly missing falling onto Ken. Then Luke cut off the pincers of the third beetle, sliced off its antennae, and zapped it right between its eyes.

"Watch out—up there!" Ken screamed, as another Fefze beetle leapt from an overhanging ledge.

It landed right on top of Luke, trapping his neck in its pincers. As Luke gasped, Ken stood by helplessly, watching in terror.

Han was too busy with the Fefze beetle in front of him to come to Luke's rescue.

"Oh, dear, oh my, someone's got to *do* something to help Master Luke!" Threepio shouted, hopping back and forth from one leg to the other.

Ken overcame his fears for the moment, and suddenly found the courage to grab the insect's pincers and pull them apart, freeing Luke from their deadly grip.

Having finished off the beetle in front of him, Han then rushed forward and finished off the last of the Fefze beetles with his blaster.

"Wow," said Ken, with a sigh of relief. "I did it,

Luke! I saved you!"

"Thanks, Ken," Luke said with relief.

Han smiled. "Good work! In a pinch—you proved yourself a real champ, Ken," he said.

Luke knelt beside the body of one of the giant beetles. "Fefze beetles never grow this large," he mused. "They've probably mutated from all of the hazardous wastes on Duro. I'll bet they were starving because all the creatures they usually eat are dying off."

After climbing over the slimy, oozing bodies of the Fefze beetles blocking the narrow gorge, Luke, Han, Threepio, and Ken finally came upon the hidden entrance to the Valley of Royalty. If they hadn't known exactly where to look, they never would have located it. It was disguised by a rocky surface, as if it were a natural part of the cliff.

Forcing open the door, they found the stairwell that descended deep into the mountain. The steep steps seemed to go on forever, fading away into the darkness.

After unpacking their portable C-beam strobe lamps, and a sharp descent of at least a thousand steps, they reached a flat tunnel that went directly below the Great Wall.

At the intersection where the passageway divided in two and split off in different directions, Luke stopped to examine the copy he had made from Dustini's hologram of the tunnels.

DRIP . . . DRIP . . . DRIP . . .

Luke looked up. A thick, gooey liquid was dripping through the rocks—right onto his map. *TSSSSSS!*

Whatever it was, it burned a hole in the map, eating through the paper quickly! Luke dropped what was left of it on the ground, before any of it got on his hands, and stepped back.

"Uh-oh," Ken said, shining his C-beam lamp on a puddle in front of them.

"The floor of this tunnel is covered with an odorous, gluelike substance," Threepio said, with alarm. "If only Artoo-Detoo were here, he'd be able to tell us the chemical makeup—"

Luke took a whiff of the puddle. "The Empire probably manufactures starship propellants above ground somewhere near here," he said. "My guess is, the chemicals are leaking through the rocks."

Suddenly there was a low rumbling sound.

PAH-BUMMMMMMMM!

A blast came from above. The tunnel trembled, shaking violently, as if struck by a huge tremor.

Then the rumbling stopped. Luke, Han, Threepio, and Ken cautiously stepped around the chemical puddle and continued along another wide, underground passageway. Soon they were completely lost. Without their map, they might continue winding through these catacombs forever and never find their way out.

Suddenly Threepio stopped in his tracks. "Excuse me, Master Luke," he said, "but I seem to detect an ultrahigh-frequency sound coming from behind the wall of this tunnel." Threepio touched the tunnel wall. "Why, these aren't ordinary rocks," he concluded. "It's just like the camouflage that covered the door up above. There is another door here. And goodness, the sounds I hear are coming from a droid on the other side. He's trying to communicate!"

"What's he saying, Threepio?" Luke asked.

"It sounds like a call for help. Oh my, I also detect a human life-form behind the door. Someone's trapped!"

Luke touched the rock facing that covered the door, moving his hand along the surface until he felt a piece of jagged rock that was sticking out farther than the rest. He then drew his lightsaber, burning through the piece of rock and exposing a lock mechanism.

Han took out his blaster and fired directly at the lock. Then Han and Luke began pushing the door up together, raising it.

SQUEEEEEEE . . .

They found themselves staring into the face of a tall, thin man dressed in the gray uniform of an Imperial prisoner. His long white hair stuck out in all directions, and he had scorch marks on his temples, as if he had been burned by a laser or electricity. Next to the man was—

"An assassin droid!" Luke shouted, pointing his lightsaber at the dangerous Imperial robot.

"Wait!" the man shouted. "Stop!" The man's eyes widened, and his eyebrows drew close together. "The droid is unarmed. He won't harm you. His violence program has been destroyed."

Luke held his lightsaber up very close to the assassin droid's chest as a warning. "Don't budge, or my lightsaber will fry your circuits to a crisp," Luke said sternly. Then he glanced at Threepio. "Threepio, check out this droid."

Threepio opened a panel on the assassin droid's back and carefully inspected its circuits.

"Harmless," Threepio concluded. "Quite harmless. Its circuits that control aggression and violent behavior are damaged, shorted out by a power surge of some kind."

"You see, it's like I told you, whoever you are," the prisoner explained, "he's harmless."

"This is Han Solo, this is Ken, and this is our droid, See-Threepio. I'm Commander Luke Skywalker of the Alliance," Luke said, looking the man over carefully.

"Skywalker. That name is not unknown to me. But the Skywalker I heard about was a Jedi Knight."

"I am a Jedi Knight," Luke replied. "We are with the Alliance."

"Then you believe in the Force," the white-haired man said. "I once knew a woman who lived by the ways of the Force. Her name was Kendalina. With bright gray eyes . . ." The man paused, looking directly at Ken. He seemed as though he wanted to say something more but then decided not to.

"What happened to Kendalina?" Ken asked.

"When the Empire discovered Kendalina was a Jedi, they destroyed her. It was a horrible day, burned into my memory forever, like these scars burned into my temples."

"You wear the clothes of an Imperial prisoner," Luke said. "Did you escape?"

"Fortunately, yes," the prisoner replied. "Defeen, the interrogator who questioned me, recommended me for a lobotomy. The Empire wished to make me docile and obedient. But I've spoiled their plans, thanks to this assassin droid here. I changed the droid's programming. Now he is my ally. At my request, he burned off the location forbidder the Empire had fastened to my wrist. Now they can no longer keep track of my every movement."

"Have you seen anyone else down here in these tunnels?" Luke asked. "We were told that there are archaeologists hiding in these caverns beneath the Valley of Royalty."

"Archaeologists, yes," the man replied. "I see everything and everyone, whether in front or behind. It's why they call me Triclops—for I have three eyes."

"Triclops!" Ken exclaimed. He was both excited and skeptical at the same time.

The man with the white hair turned his head, revealing an eye in the back of his skull—a powerful eye that seemed to send out hypnotic waves, making Ken blink and feel dizzy.

Ken looked away quickly, short of breath.

"He really *is* Triclops!" the young Jedi Prince exclaimed. "Trioculus only *pretended* to be the son of Emperor Palpatine. His third eye was on his forehead. But the real son of the Emperor has a third eye on the *back* of his head, just like you."

"Yes, just like me," Triclops repeated, turning around to face front once again. He looked at Ken with his two front eyes. "I remember Trioculus well. And a merciless slavemaster he was. When I was a patient in the Imperial insane asylum, back in the spice mines of Kessel, he used to whip me. And with every lash of the whip he swore that one day he would assume my identity—once Palpatine died he would convince the entire galaxy that *he* was the Emperor's true three-eyed son. Then he would take over as ruler of the Empire!"

"He was the ruler of the Empire for awhile," Ken said. "But now he's frozen in carbonite and hanging in a museum in Cloud City."

"You know a great deal," Triclops said. Then he reached out and touched the semi-transparent, silvery crystal that Ken wore around his neck. "Who gave this to you?" he said slowly, with reflection.

Ken backed away, pushing Triclops's hand from the crystal. "I don't know. I've always had it, ever since I was little."

"Always is a long time, even for someone so young." Triclops pointed to the scars on his temples. "Seems like I've always had *these*. The Empire began shock therapy on me when *I* was young. But lightning bolts, with energy from the Dark Side, never conquered me. And now I've escaped from the Empire at last. With help from this assassin droid, I climbed down the mouth of the monument of Queen Rana. I would have found my way to freedom, but I got trapped down here in these tunnels."

Triclops closed all three of his eyes and began rubbing his temples. Then he opened his eyes and said, "Well, so it's archaeologists you want, is it? Come, I will lead you to them."

"Or perhaps you intend to lead us into a trap," Luke mused.

"You live by the ways of the Force, don't you, Jedi?" Triclops said, frowning. "Consult the Force and discover whether I lead you into a trap—or whether I am about to lead you to your goal."

CHAPTER 8
The Imperial Attack

Luke accepted Triclops's challenge.

As he concentrated on the Force, he felt a feeling of trust; but he also felt confusion rather than certainty.

"Of course you trust me," Triclops said, "I've always despised the Empire. The Empire considers *me* hopelessly insane." Triclops tapped a forefinger against his forehead. "But wanting to destroy the Empire hardly qualifies me as crazy or insane, wouldn't you agree?"

At that, Triclops and the assassin droid led Luke, Han, Threepio, and Ken on a twisting, winding path through the musty tunnel. Luke kept his guard up the whole way, holding his lightsaber with its blade glowing, ready to use at a moment's notice.

The group soon emerged into a wide cavern. There they beheld a dazzling display of ancient treasures. A team of thirteen Duro aliens was hard at work. Dustini had said that their group consisted of fifteen archaeologists, including himself. That meant that one of them was unaccounted for, at least for the moment.

Antigravity carts were piled high with crates filled with scrolls, statues, ornaments, vases, jewelry, masks, ancient costumes, coins—every type of relic imaginable. The carts glided smoothly, without any wheels, floating back and forth above the ground.

The work of the archaeologists, however, seemed far from done.

Luke put away his lightsaber. "Greetings from SPIN!" he shouted, stepping out from behind a boulder to reveal himself. Threepio poked his head out next, followed by Han and Ken. Triclops and his assassin droid remained in the shadows. "Don't be frightened," Luke continued. "Dustini sent us to rescue you."

Upon hearing Dustini's name the archaeologists gathered around and activated their translators to communicate. Their gray-skinned faces showed great relief as they listened to Luke's words.

To Han Solo's embarrassment, one of the Duro aliens even hugged him.

"Easy does it," Han said. "I'm a Corellian, and we Corellians gave up hugging strangers four centuries ago."

Another archaeologist dropped to his knees, thanking them and shouting praises to Dustini for having sent help. "I'm Dustangle," he explained. "Dustini is my cousin, but he has always been more like a brother to me. We're grateful he sent you to help us. We must leave our native planet. It has become a wasteland. But we can't leave our treasures

here. These treasures hold the memories and the history of our people. They must be protected for future generations. They must not fall into the hands of Kadann."

"We've landed our transport vehicle in the mountains beyond the Valley of Royalty," Luke explained to Dustangle. "It's large enough to hold most, if not all of your relics. If you wish, SPIN will protect them at Mount Yoda, on behalf of all Duros, until your people relocate in safety without fear of destruction from the Empire."

They started right away to move the archaeological treasures down the tunnel. The antigravity carts were designed so that they could be gently pushed up the winding stairs that led to the planet's surface.

Everyone helped—Triclops and the assassin droid, and even See-Threepio pitched in.

After lifting a crate onto one of the carts, Ken accidentally knocked over a small emerald box containing a collection of ancient rings. Han helped pick up the jewelry and put it back in its case.

Dustangle noticed a ring that Han left behind. He reached down to pick it up.

"It's an ancient wedding ring," Dustangle explained, handing it to Han. "It belonged to a Corellian Princess who was a friend of our Queen Rana. You're a Corellian who's come to save us, so from now on, the ring shall belong to you. Please accept it as a sign of our gratitude. Perhaps some day you'll give it to the one you love, on the day that you get married."

Han blushed. "Marriage isn't exactly in my plans right at the moment," he explained, "but, well . . . who knows?"

Han winked, then pocketed the ring thoughtfully.

Above ground, inside the Imperial Reprogramming Institute, piercing red eyes shone brightly from the wolflike face of Defeen.

Defeen, the Imperial interrogator, held several truth needles tightly between his vicious yellow claws.

He drooled with excitement. In just a few moments the Empire would learn once and for all the exact location where the archaeologists were hiding underground. And then perhaps Defeen would be considered for yet another promotion. The Defel alien

relished the thought of gaining more power within the Empire, hopefully one day leaving the Imperial Reprogramming Institute for a truly important position, perhaps one at Emperor Kadann's side.

"Sssssssspeak!" Defeen hissed, baring his white fangs at the Duro archaeologist fastened to the interrogation table. "You will sssssssspeak!"

The Duro archaeologist had been captured by Imperial intelligence agents when he had tried to escape the planet, like Dustini. Although his situation looked grim, he was determined not to betray his people.

"Evvvvverything! You will tell me evvvverything about where your friends are hiding!"

The Empire had heard stories about the cavern that was hidden deep beneath the Valley of Royalty—but where could it be exactly? And how could they find it?

The archaeologist refused to speak.

"All riiiiiiight, then . . ."

With that, Defeen pushed two needles into the truth centers of his victim's brain.

The archaeologist gasped and closed his eyes, shaking his head back and forth. But the truth needles were too powerful. "Through the mouth of Queen Rana's Face, a tunnel down to the catacombs . . . the cavern, seventeen paces to the left of the face . . . fifteen standard units beneath the ground . . . that's where they've collected the relics of Duro . . ."

"So you talk at lasssssst!" Defeen said, with a sneer.

* * *

Without delay the Imperials moved a powerful device resembling a giant drill to a position seventeen paces to the left of Queen Rana's face. Known as a zenomach, the ground-boring machine was set to plunge fifteen standard units beneath the Valley of Royalty.

ZIIIIIIIIIIICH!

The ground nearly disintegrated under the force of the powerful zenomach. Rocks crumbled, dirt swirled, and a hole began to appear, large enough for Imperial stormtroopers to descend into the catacombs below.

RUMMMMMMMMMMBLE . . .

The ground shook furiously as the zenomach unexpectedly set off forceful ground tremors. It was a large quake that reached 77.88 on the Imperial quake scale.

When the tremors stopped, High Prophet Jedgar glanced down into the hole in the ground. He could clearly see that fifteen standard units below they had broken through the roof of a cavern. Light streamed through the hole, glinting off some golden relics. It was just a hint of the many treasures down below, but Jedgar couldn't wait to take them back to Space Station Scardia and add them to Kadann's already enormous collection.

High Prophet Jedgar grabbed hold of one of the ladders attached to a flex-mount. The flex-mount instantly lowered twistable ladders into a deep hole, allowing entry into otherwise inaccessible areas.

The Imperials began to descend, with Grand Moff Hissa and High Prophet Jedgar following close behind the first exploratory force of stormtroopers.

Luke, Han, and the Duro archaeologists counterattacked, and a battle ensued.

As his eyes adjusted to the dim, golden glow of the archaeologists' cavern, High Prophet Jedgar spied Ken. Noticing the silvery crystal the boy wore on a chain around his neck, Jedgar wondered whether this was the Jedi Prince whom Trioculus had failed to find and destroy. According to legend, the Jedi Prince wore a dome-shaped birthstone on a necklace chain, and he had worn it all his life—ever since the boy was first taken to the Lost City of the Jedi to be raised by droids.

"Take that boy hostage, Hissa—at once!" Jedgar demanded.

Grand Moff Hissa clutched Ken.

"Let go of me!" the Jedi Prince shouted, as Hissa pressed a laserblaster against the boy's chin. Ken stopped squirming and held very still.

"Good work, Hissa," Jedgar said.

Hearing Ken's shout for help, Luke Skywalker hurriedly pushed two stormtroopers aside and pointed his lightsaber at the grand moff, ready to put an end to Hissa as swiftly as he had destroyed the attacking giant Fefze beetles.

"Drop your weapon, or I'll destroy the boy—now!" Grand Moff Hissa exclaimed.

Luke hesitated. The grand moff tightened his grip on his laserblaster.

"Now, Skywalker!" High Prophet Jedgar demanded, reinforcing Hissa's order.

Beads of sweat ran down Luke's brow as he retracted his lightsaber and dropped the weapon to the ground.

"Very good, Skywalker," Hissa said, gnashing his pointed teeth. "Now prepare to join your master, Obi-Wan Kenobi, in the world beyond!"

Breathing fast, Ken's mind was spinning with confusion and fear. Locked in Grand Moff Hissa's tight grasp, Ken saw Triclops glancing out from behind a boulder, looking at him intently and nodding. Triclops suddenly turned his head around and stared at Grand Moff Hissa with the eye at the back of his skull. An incredibly strong magnetic force seemed to flow out of Triclops's third eye, as a power beam tugged at Hissa.

Overcome by surprise, the grand moff loosened his grip on Ken. He was yanked off his feet and violently pulled toward Triclops.

Triclops quickly spun around to face Hissa, grabbing the grand moff by the neck and knocking the blaster out of his hand. Hissa tried to bite Triclops with his razor-sharp teeth, but Triclops squeezed with his long fingers, causing Hissa to gasp and choke.

"You won't let a pacifist live in peace," Triclops scolded sternly. "You're forcing me to abandon my

principles."

RUMMMMMMMMMMBLE!

The cavern swayed as another tremor struck.

KRAAAAAAAAKK!

High above them the dam, looming beyond the Valley of Royalty, split under the force of the latest quake. A lake of thick, fuming liquid burst through the cracked dam, flowing and oozing across the valley like a foul-smelling tidal wave.

The rapids raced across the ground, quickly arriving at the hole the zenomach had bored.

As the gooey, hazardous liquids poured into the hole, Triclops released his grip on Hissa. The grand moff crumpled onto the ground, and Triclops retreated from his victim. With the eye in the back of his head, Triclops saw that Grand Moff Hissa, now screaming and grasping for help, lay directly in the path of the bubbling, burning liquid.

TSSSSSSSS . . .

Acid flowed over Grand Moff Hissa's legs. Hissa thrashed helplessly, trying to remove himself from the path of the dangerous chemicals. "Ahhhhhhhrrrrrgggh!" the grand moff screamed. "Help, Jedgar, help!"

Hissa tried to prop himself up, but his arms slid right into the toxic chemicals.

"Noooooo, Jedgarrrrr!" he cried at the top of his lungs.

Grand Moff Hissa's arms began to melt. "Don't leave me here to die!" he shouted.

Ken covered his eyes but peeked through his closed fingers to look at Hissa one last time. There was little left of Hissa's arms and legs, though the grand moff's head, chest, and waist still twisted and writhed on the cavern floor.

High Prophet Jedgar was more concerned about saving his own life than in assisting what little was left of Grand Moff Hissa. As the toxic liquid spread through the cavern and surged like floodwaters into the tunnels, Jedgar fled, followed by Imperial stormtroopers who were still firing at Luke and Han. The stormtroopers broke ranks and scattered.

Triclops's assassin droid was struck by a blast from a stormtrooper's portable laser cannon. His metal parts shattered, hurled everywhere from the cavern ceiling to the craggy floor.

Riding antigravity carts through the tunnels, Luke, Han, Ken, Threepio, Triclops, and the Duro archaeologists finally reached the stairwell, in advance of the deadly flow. The crates with relics were then hastily transported up the tunnel stairwell inside the mountain, all the way to the surface where they were to be stowed aboard the transport ship.

"I've got a really bad feeling about this," Han said, as he suddenly realized that the transport ship

was no longer where they had left it.

"Oh dear, perhaps some Imperials ambushed the ship and took it, with Princess Leia and Chewbacca inside," Threepio exclaimed, waving his arms wildly in dismay.

But the Corellian Transport suddenly came into view through the thick clouds above the mountains. Leia guided the ship back into the valley for a smooth landing, with Chewbacca copiloting.

The moment Luke climbed up the ramp and boarded the ship, Leia hugged her brother. "Luke, you're safe!" she exclaimed. "And so are we, but just barely. An Imperial probe droid flew overhead and spotted us just after you left. We blasted off to take it out of action."

"We'd better get this ship off the ground fast," Han said, as the archaeologists stowed their crates of relics onto the transport ship, "before any Imperials find us and realize we've filled the storage hold with the treasures of Duro."

"Han and I will navigate, Chewie," Princess Leia said. "I think Han still doesn't believe how well I can fly a Corellian Action VI Transport spaceship. Shall I show him?"

"Grooooarf!" Chewbacca agreed, tucking his furry hands behind his head and putting his feet up on the console.

Han gave Leia a kiss on the cheek. "Are you ready, copilot?" he asked her. "Go ahead and power up."

As the ship lifted from the ground, it tipped and vibrated from all the weight now aboard. Never had a Corellian Action VI Transport been so packed, from the cargo hold all the way to the passenger lounge.

"I want you to know," Triclops said, sitting next to Luke, "that if the day ever comes that I sit upon the Imperial throne as my father did, I'll force the Empire to pay for what it did to the planet Duro. I'll take the Empire apart, brigade by brigade, one mechanized army at a time, until the Dark Side is completely powerless."

"That's a nice dream," Luke said.

"My dreams shall become real," Triclops replied.

"You've helped us so far," Luke said. "Still, you'll have to prove yourself to the Alliance. Mon Mothma will have to keep you under guard, I'm afraid, until she's convinced beyond any doubt that you're not a spy."

But Triclops was no longer listening. All three of his eyes were now closed, and he drifted off, falling into a deep sleep.

A few days later, the misty clouds of Dagobah parted as two spaceships came zooming toward the peak of Mount Yoda: the *Millennium Falcon*, which had been fully repaired at Orbiting Shipyard Alpha, and the Corellian Action VI Transport with the treasures of Duro aboard.

At the landing pad the members of the returning mission from Mount Yoda were greeted by Mon Mothma and Ken's personal droid, Chip. As Luke had warned, guards surrounded Triclops and took him in custody for observation. Triclops did not resist. To Luke and Leia's astonishment, they then saw

Dustini walking briskly over to them from the main DRAPAC building.

Having recovered with the help of Alliance medical droids, Dustini hugged Dustangle and the other Duro archaeologists. As he beheld the storehouse of treasures in the cargo hold, Dustini's eyes widened in amazement.

"Thank you, Luke—thank you, everyone!" Dustini said. "Now the history of our planet Duro will be preserved, to be studied by future generations."

"Speaking of study," Chip said, putting his hands on his metallic hips, "I see that our truant student has finally returned to start school at Dagobah Tech."

"Missing school was an accident, Chip," Ken replied. "I couldn't help it."

"A likely story," Chip said sternly. "A very likely story indeed."

As the guards took Triclops toward an entrance into DRAPAC, Ken glanced at the Imperial prisoner. Ken couldn't help but wonder why the Empire had decided to keep Triclops alive for all these years, especially since the Empire considered him to be such a threat.

Could Triclops prove to be a threat to the Alliance as well? Were these really the last days of the Alliance, as in Kadann's recent prophecy?

When the dragon pack,
Perched upon Yoda's stony back,

Receives a visitor pierced by gold,
Then come the last days of the Rebel Alliance.

A visitor had been pierced by gold. And now the son of the evil Emperor Palpatine was in their midst, claiming to be a pacifist who wanted to destroy his father's Empire.

It was all too troublesome for a boy of twelve to dwell on, especially when Leia distracted him by reaching over and mussing up his moppy brown hair.

Ken and Leia both grinned, breaking into wide smiles at the same instant. It was a good feeling, Ken thought—to be back with all his friends from SPIN, sheltered at the mountaintop fortress on the planet that the wise Jedi master Yoda once called home. It was a good feeling indeed.

To find out more about Triclops, and about Kadann's conflict with the Imperial grand moffs and the affect on Han and Leia's plans for their future, don't miss *Queen of the Empire,* book five of our continuing Star Wars adventures.

Here's a preview:

"Next stop, Hologram Fun World!" Han said, as he navigated the *Millennium Falcon* to avoid an asteroid.

"We can't go to Hologram Fun World, Han," Leia protested. "We've got work to do for SPIN back at Mount Yoda. We don't have time to waste."

"Who said we were going to waste time?" Han said. And then, just like that, he blurted out, "We're going to elope!"

"Are you asking me to marry you, Han?" Leia asked.

"I guess you could look at it that way, if you want," Han said. "I mean, that's what it usually means to elope, doesn't it? To fly off somewhere in a hurry and get, and get, you know ..." Han gave a deep sigh and continued. "Don't act as if this comes as such a big shock, okay? I just started thinking, I guess."

"Thinking about me?" Leia asked.

"Thinking about the fact that I'm not getting any younger, and that if I ever want any pip-squeak Solo kids running around my sky house tugging at my boots, well, it just wouldn't seem right unless you were their mother." He gazed into her eyes. "Does that make any sense?"

"Perfect sense," she answered.

"You look lovely, my dear," said the Imperial tyrant, thrusting out his chest in military fashion. "And the moment you've secretly dreamed of for so long has now arrived. Princess Leia, you're about to become my bride!"

He withdrew his right hand from behind his back, revealing a dozen black zinthorn flowers. "For you," he said. "A wedding bouquet!"

Leia accepted the horrible zinthorns. The grand moff, who was to perform the wedding ceremony, opened the Dark Book of Imperial Justice and began reading aloud. "We are witnesses to a momentous event," he began, "the marriage of our Imperial ruler to Princess Leia Organa, who shall now of her own free will renounce the Rebel Alliance and offer her eternal allegiance to the Dark Side! Thus, Leia will prepare herself to follow in the path of her father, Darth Vader, and at last shall become our queen!"

Can Princess Leia resist the Emperor's attempt to lure her to the Dark Side? And what menace unfolds when Zorba the Hutt meets up with Han and Leia at Hologram Fun World, the most incredible theme park in the galaxy? Find out in *Queen of the Empire*, coming soon.

Glossary

Assassin droid
A very menacing and dangerous Imperial droid designed to carry out assassinations. An assassin droid assists Triclops in his escape from the Imperial Reprogramming Institute.

Carbonite
A substance made from Tibanna gas, plentiful on the planet Bespin, where it is mined and sold in liquid form as a fuel in Cloud City. When carbonite is turned into a solid, it can be used for keeping humans or other organisms alive in a state of suspended animation, encasing them completely. Zorba the Hutt encased Trioculus in carbonite, just as Darth Vader did to Han Solo in *The Empire Strikes Back*.

Chief Muskov
Chief of the Cloud Police of Cloud City.

Chip (short for Microchip)
Ken's personal droid, who lived with him in the Lost City of the Jedi and has now gone out into the world with him.

Corellian Action VI Transport
A space transport that Han and Chewbacca pilot from Orbiting Shipyard Alpha to the surface of the planet Duro.

Defeen

A cunning, sharp-clawed Defel alien. Defeen is an interrogator first class at the Imperial Reprogramming Institute in the Valley of Royalty on the planet Duro.

DRAPAC

A new Rebel Alliance center, built at the peak of Mount Yoda on Dagobah, the planet where the Jedi Master Yoda lived. DRAPAC stands for Defense Research and Planetary Assistance Center. This Alliance installation has become SPIN's most well defended fortress.

Duro

A planet that had a grand history, especially during its Golden Age, but which now is being used by the Empire as a toxic waste dump and the site of its Imperial Reprogramming Institute.

Dustangle

An alien archaeologist who's in hiding in the underground caverns of Duro. He's a cousin of Dustini.

Dustini

An alien archaeologist from the planet Duro, Dustini makes a voyage to get help from the Alliance.

Emperor Palpatine

Now deceased, Emperor Palpatine was once a senator in the Old Republic, but he destroyed the old democratic order and established the ruthless Galactic Empire in its place. Palpatine ruled the galaxy with military might and tyranny, forcing human and alien citizens of every planet to live in fear. He was assisted by Darth Vader, who eventually turned against him, hurling the Emperor to his death in the power core of the Death Star. Triclops, his three-eyed son, is considered insane by the Empire and kept imprisoned in Imperial asylums.

Grand Moff Hissa
The Imperial grand moff (high-ranking Imperial governor) whom Trioculus trusts the most. He has spear-pointed teeth and is now in command of the grand moffs.

High Prophet Jedgar
A seven-foot-tall prophet whom Kadann, the Supreme Prophet of the Dark Side, most relies upon to help fulfill his prophecies and commands.

Kadann
A black-bearded dwarf, Kadann is the Supreme Prophet of the Dark Side. The Prophets of the Dark Side are a group of Imperials who, while posing as being very mystical, are actually a sort of Imperial Bureau of Investigation with its own network of spies.

Kadann prophesied that the next Emperor would wear the glove of Darth Vader. Kadann's prophecies are mysterious four-line, nonrhyming verses. They are carefully studied by the Rebel Alliance for clues about what the Empire might be planning.

Kate (short for KT-18)
A female, pearl-colored housekeeping droid that Luke bought from jawas on Tatooine as a housewarming gift for Han Solo.

Ken
A twelve-year-old Jedi Prince who was raised by droids in the Lost City of the Jedi after being brought to the underground city as a small child by a Jedi Knight in a brown robe. He knows nothing of his origins, but he does know many Imperial secrets, which he learned from studying the files of the master Jedi computer in the Jedi Library where he went to school. Long an admirer of Luke Skywalker, he has departed the Lost City and joined the Alliance.

Mon Mothma
A distinguished-looking leader, she has long been in charge of the Rebel Alliance.

Mount Yoda
A mountain on the planet Dagobah, named in honor of the late Jedi Master, Yoda. This is the site where the Rebel Alliance has built DRAPAC, their new Defense Research and Planetary Assistance Center.

Orbiting Shipyard Alpha
A spaceship repair dock that orbits the planet Duro.

Prophets of the Dark Side
A sort of Imperial Bureau of Investigation run by black-bearded prophets who work within a network of spies. The prophets have much power within the Empire. To retain their control, they make sure their prophecies come true—even if it takes force, bribery, or murder.

Queen Rana
An ancient queen of Duro. There's a large monument to

Queen Rana in the Valley of Royalty.

Scardia Voyager
The gold-colored spaceship of the Prophets of the Dark Side.

Septapus
Ocean creatures with seven tentacles and five glowing eyes, septapuses are said to be harmless vegetarians, though Han Solo claims he was once viciously attacked by one.

Space Station Scardia
A cube-shaped space station where the Prophets of the Dark Side live.

Triclops
The true mutant, three-eyed son of the late Emperor Palpatine. Triclops has spent most of his life in Imperial insane asylums, and was recently moved to the Imperial Reprogramming Institute on the planet Duro. He has two eyes on the front of his head and one on the back. He has scars on his temples from shock treatments, and his hair is white and jagged, sticking out in all directions. Considered insane by the Empire, Triclops has a serene, peaceful look with quiet, iron determination.

Trioculus
A three-eyed mutant who was the Supreme Slavelord of Kessel. He was encased in carbonite by Zorba the Hutt. Trioculus is a liar and impostor who claims to be the son of Emperor Palpatine. In his rise to power as Emperor, he

was supported by the grand moffs, who helped him find the glove of Darth Vader, an everlasting symbol of evil.

Valley of Royalty
A famous valley on the planet Duro, surrounded by a large stone wall. The Valley of Royalty is the site of monuments to many of Duro's ancient kings and queens, such as Queen Rana.

Yoda
The Jedi Master Yoda was a small creature who lived on the bog planet Dagobah. For eight hundred years before passing away he taught Jedi Knights, including Obi-Wan Kenobi and Luke Skywalker, in the ways of the Force.

Zenomach
A ground-boring machine of great power, much like a giant drill.

Zorba the Hutt
The father of Jabba the Hutt. A sluglike creature with a long braided white beard, Zorba is now the ruling Governor of Cloud City. He expelled Lando Calrissian from that post, after having beaten Lando in a rigged card game of sabacc in the Holiday Towers Hotel and Casino.

Z'trop
The planet Z'trop is an extremely scenic and romantic tropical world. Noted for its pleasant volcanic islands, it has wide beaches and clear waters. Han and Leia vacation on Z'trop with Luke, Ken, Chewbacca, and the droids after *Zorba the Hutt's Revenge*.

About the Authors

PAUL DAVIDS is a graduate of Princeton and the American Film Institute Center for Advanced Film Studies. His screenwriting credits include the critically acclaimed feature *She Dances Alone* starring Bud Cort and Max von Sydow. He is also an executive producer of a dramatic motion picture for HBO based on the book *UFO Crash at Roswell*.

Mr. Davids was production coordinator and a writer of the TV series, *The Transformers*, as well as a writer for *Defenders of the Earth*, *C.O.P.S.*, *The Spiral Zone*, and *The Bionic Six*. His first book, *The Fires of Pele: Mark Twain's Legendary Lost Journal*, was coauthored by his wife, Hollace. Now they are hard at work on even more Star Wars books for young readers.

HOLLACE DAVIDS is a graduate of Goucher and received a master's degree in counseling at Boston University. After teaching children with learning disabilities, she worked for the L.A. International Film Exposition and went on to become a publicist. For more than a decade she has overseen premieres for the release of most of Columbia's and now TriStar Pictures's feature films. Currently she is vice-president of publicity and special events for TriStar Pictures.

Whether it's because they grew up in nearby hometowns (Hollace is from Silver Spring, Maryland, and Paul is from Bethesda), or because they share many common interests, collaboration comes naturally to them — both in their writing and in raising a family. The Davids have a daughter, Jordan, and a son, Scott.

About the Illustrators

JUNE BRIGMAN was born in 1960 in Atlanta, Georgia, and has been drawing since she was old enough to hold a pencil. She studied art at the University of Georgia and Georgia State University, but her illustrations are based on real-life observation and skills she developed over a summer as a pastel portrait artist at Six Flags Over Georgia amusement park, when she was only sixteen. At twenty she discovered comic books at a comic convention, and by the time she was twenty-two she got her first job working for Marvel Comics, where she created the *Power Pack* series. A devout horse enthusiast and Bruce Springsteen fan, Ms. Brigman lives and works in White Plains, New York.

KARL KESEL was born in 1959 and raised in the small town of Victor, New York. He started reading comic books at the age of ten, while traveling cross-country with his family, and decided soon after that he wanted to become a cartoonist. By the age of twenty-five, he landed a full-time job as an illustrator for DC Comics, working on such titles as *Superman*, *World's Finest*, *Newsboy Legion*, and *Hawk and Dove*, which he also cowrote. He was also one of the artists on the *Terminator* and *Indiana Jones* miniseries for Dark Horse Comics. Mr. Kesel lives and works with his wife, Barbara, in Milwaukie, Oregon.

DREW STRUZAN is a teacher, lecturer, and one of the most influential forces working in commercial art today. His strong visual sense and recognizable style have produced lasting pieces of art for advertising, the recording industry, and motion pictures. His paintings include the album covers for *Alice Cooper's Greatest Hits* and *Welcome to My Nightmare*, which was recently voted one of the one hundred classic album covers of all time by *Rolling Stone* magazine. He has also created the movie posters for Star Wars, *E.T. The Extra-Terrestrial*, the Back to the Future series, the Indiana Jones series, *An American Tale*, and *Hook*. Mr. Struzan lives and works in the California valley with his wife, Cheryle. Their son, Christian, is continuing in the family tradition, working as an art director and illustrator.